"Colors are the music of the eyes."

— Eugène Delacroix

The author wishes to thank Bernard Bonnet, Gwendolyn H. Goffe, Diane Lovejoy, and Patricia Smith.

© 2003 by The Museum of Fine Arts, Houston

Creative direction and design: Caroline Desnoëttes
Typography and production: Ashley Edwards and Phenon Finley-Smiley
Photography: Thomas R. DuBrock and Laura Nelson Wells
Color separations, printing, and binding: Arti Grafiche Amilcare Pizzi
Printed in Italy
ISBN: 0-89090-121-X

Caroline Desnoëttes

COLORS

of The Museum of Fine Arts, Houston

The Museum of Fine Arts, Houston

The Artists' Palette

Childe Hassam
Evening in New York, 1890s
Pages 4–5

Paul Cézanne
Bottom of the Ravine, c. 1879
Pages 14–15

Frederick Judd Waugh
Mid Ocean, n.d.
Pages 24–25

Henri Manguin
The Port of Saint-Tropez, 1905
Pages 6–7

George Bellows
Portrait of Florence Pierce, 1914
Pages 16–17

Vincent van Gogh
The Rocks, 1888
Pages 26–27

Henri Matisse
Woman in a Purple Coat, 1937
Pages 8–9

Gustave Caillebotte
The Orange Trees, 1878
Pages 18–19

Paul Sérusier
Landscape at Le Pouldu, 1890
Pages 28–29

Burgoyne Diller
Abstraction, 1934
Pages 10–11

Paul Signac
The Bonaventure Pine, 1893
Pages 20–21

František Kupka
The Yellow Scale, c. 1907
Pages 30–31

Paul Klee
Marjamshausen, 1928
Pages 12–13

**Dorothy Antoinette
(Toni) LaSelle**
Puritan, 1947–50
Pages 22–23

Kermit Oliver
K.J.'s Calf, 1975
Pages 32–33

E. Martin Hennings
Passing By, c. 1924
Pages 34–35

Roger de la Fresnaye
The Fourteenth of July, 1914
Pages 44–45

William Bouguereau
The Elder Sister, 1869
Pages 54–55

Auguste Renoir
Still Life with Bouquet, 1871
Pages 36–37

Alexei Jawlensky
Portrait of a Woman, 1912
Pages 46–47

Frederic Remington
Aiding a Comrade
(Past All Surgery), 1889–90
Pages 56–57

André Derain
The Turning Road,
L'Estaque, 1906
Pages 38–39

Susan Rothenberg
Red Banner, 1979
Pages 48–49

Willem Claesz. Heda
Banquet Piece with Ham, 1656
Pages 58–59

Walter Ufer
Portrait of a Man with a Pumpkin,
c. 1914–29
Pages 40–41

Kees van Dongen
The Corn Poppy, c. 1919
Pages 50–51

Henri Edmond Cross
Sunset on the Lagoon,
Venice, c. 1903–4
Pages 60–61

Georgia O'Keeffe
Red Hills with White Shell, 1938
Pages 42–43

Jean-Siméon Chardin
The Good Education, c. 1753
Pages 52–53

William Merritt Chase
Mother and Child
(The First Portrait), c. 1888
Pages 62–63

Parma violet

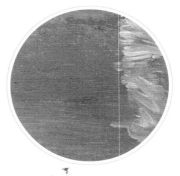

Childe Hassam
Evening in New York, 1890s
Oil on canvas, 21 $^1/_4$ x 18 $^1/_4$
Gift of Mrs. Langdon Dearborn

Mauve

Henri Manguin
The Port of Saint-Tropez, 1905
Oil on canvas, 24 x 19 3/4
Gift of Audrey Jones Beck

Purple

Henri Matisse
Woman in a Purple Coat, 1937
Oil on canvas, 31 $^{7}/_{8}$ x 25 $^{11}/_{16}$
Gift of Audrey Jones Beck

Indigo

Burgoyne Diller
Abstraction, 1934
Oil on canvas, 20 x 30
Gift of Ron and Jane Lerner

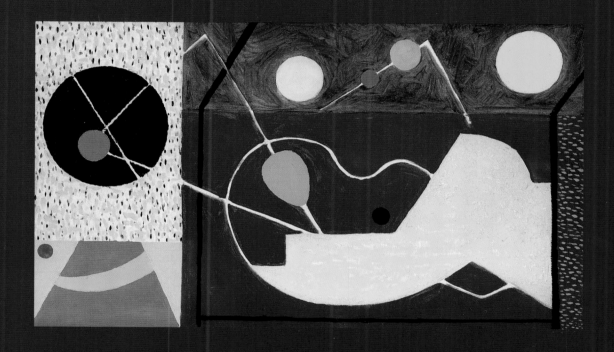

Ultramarine blue

Paul Klee
Marjamshausen, 1928
Watercolor on paper, 14 $^3/_{16}$ x 8 $^1/_{16}$
Gift of Miss Ima Hogg

Azure blue

Paul Cézanne
Bottom of the Ravine, *c. 1879*
Oil on canvas, 28 3/4 x 21 1/4
Gift of Audrey Jones Beck

Cobalt blue

George Bellows
Portrait of Florence Pierce, 1914
Oil on wood panel, 38 x 30
Gift of Mr. and Mrs. Meredith Long in
memory of Mrs. Agnes Cullen Arnold

Gray blue

Gustave Caillebotte
The Orange Trees, 1878
Oil on canvas, 61 x 46
Gift of Audrey Jones Beck

Green blue

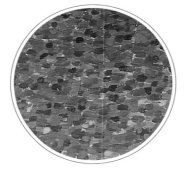

Paul Signac
***The Bonaventure Pine,* 1893**
Oil on canvas, 25 $^7/_8$ x 31 $^7/_8$
Gift of Audrey Jones Beck

Emerald green

Dorothy Antoinette (Toni) LaSelle
Puritan, 1947–50
Oil on canvas, 25 x 30
Museum purchase with funds provided by
the Frank Freed Memorial Painting Fund

Sea green

Frederick Judd Waugh
Mid Ocean, n.d.
Oil on canvas, 40 x 50 $\frac{1}{4}$
Gift of Mrs. William Stamps Farish

Moss green

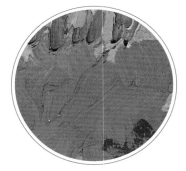

Vincent van Gogh
The Rocks, 1888
Oil on canvas, 21 5/8 x 25 7/8
Gift of Audrey Jones Beck

Meadow green

Paul Sérusier
Landscape at Le Pouldu, 1890
Oil on canvas, 29 1/4 x 36 1/4
Gift of Alice C. Simkins in memory of Alice Nicholson Hanszen

P. Sérusier – 1890

Golden yellow

František Kupka
The Yellow Scale, c. 1907
Oil on canvas, 31 x 29 ¹/₄
Gift of Audrey Jones Beck

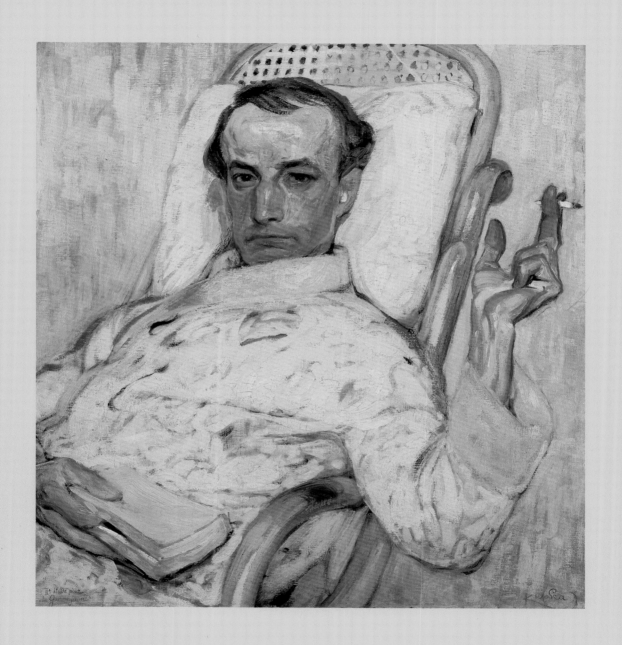

Straw yellow

Kermit Oliver
K.J.'s Calf, 1975
Acrylic on Masonite, 24 3/8 x 48
Museum purchase with funds provided by an anonymous
donor at "One Great Night in November, 1991"

Maize yellow

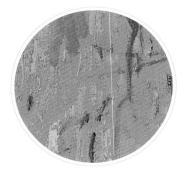

E. Martin Hennings
Passing By, c. 1924
Oil on canvas, 44 x 49
Gift of the Ranger Fund, National Academy of Design

Sienna earth

Auguste Renoir
Still Life with Bouquet, 1871
Oil on canvas, 28 $^{13}/_{16}$ x 23 $^{3}/_{16}$
The Robert Lee Blaffer Memorial Collection,
gift of Sarah Campbell Blaffer

Orange

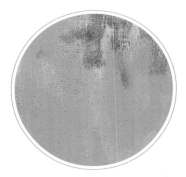

André Derain
The Turning Road, L'Estaque, *1906*
Oil on canvas, 51 x 76 ³/₄
Gift of Audrey Jones Beck

Salmon pink

Walter Ufer
Portrait of a Man with a Pumpkin, c. 1914–29
Oil on canvas, 36 x 30
Gift of General and Mrs. Maurice Hirsch

Pale pink

Georgia O'Keeffe
***Red Hills with White Shell**, 1938*
Oil on canvas, 30 x 36 ¹/₂
Gift of Isabel B. Wilson in memory of her mother, Alice Pratt Brown

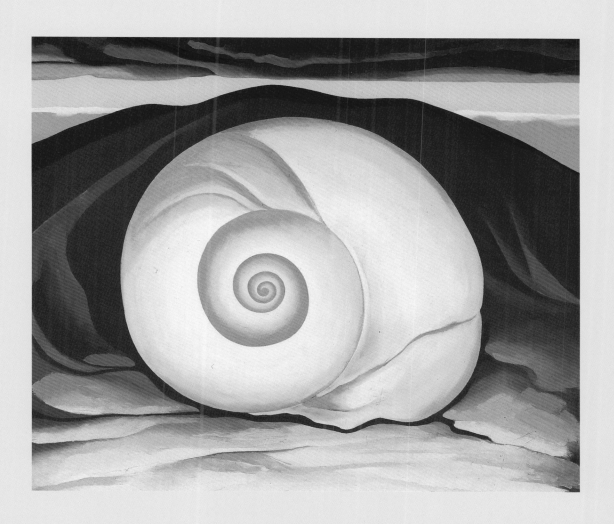

Pink

Roger de la Fresnaye
The Fourteenth of July, 1914
Oil on canvas, 28 $^1/_4$ x 38 $^1/_4$
Gift of Audrey Jones Beck

Madder red

Alexei Jawlensky
Portrait of a Woman, 1912
Oil on board, 20 $^7/_8$ x 19 $^1/_2$
Gift of Audrey Jones Beck

Carmine red

Susan Rothenberg
Red Banner, 1979
Acrylic on canvas, 90 x 123 $^7/_8$
Museum purchase with funds provided by the
National Endowment for the Arts and Caroline Wiess Law

Vermilion red

Kees van Dongen
The Corn Poppy, c. 1919
Oil on canvas, 21 $^{1}/_{2}$ x 18
Gift of Audrey Jones Beck

Sepia

Jean-Siméon Chardin
The Good Education, c. 1753
Oil on canvas, 16 5/16 x 18 5/8
Gift in memory of George R. Brown by his wife and children

Burnt umber

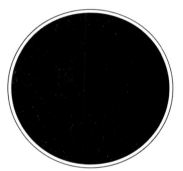

William Bouguereau
The Elder Sister, 1869
Oil on canvas, 51 $^1/_4$ x 38 $^1/_4$
Gift of an Anonymous Lady in memory of her father

W. BOVGVERLAG 1869

Sand

Frederic Remington
Aiding a Comrade (Past All Surgery), 1889–90
Oil on canvas, 34 x 48 ¹/₈
The Hogg Brothers Collection, gift of Miss Ima Hogg

Gray

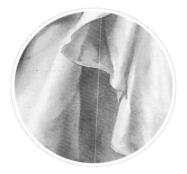

Willem Claesz. Heda
Banquet Piece with Ham, 1656
Oil on canvas, 44 x 60
Gift of Mr. and Mrs. Raymond H. Goodrich

White

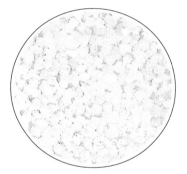

Henri Edmond Cross
Sunset on the Lagoon, Venice, *c. 1903–4*
Oil on canvas, 19 1/2 x 25 5/8
Gift of Audrey Jones Beck

Black

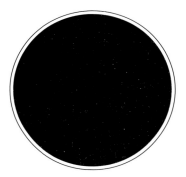

William Merritt Chase
Mother and Child (The First Portrait), c. 1888
Oil on canvas, 70 1/8 x 40 1/8
Gift of Ehrich Newhouse Gallery, New York

About the Author

Caroline Desnoëttes is a French painter who lives and works in Paris.

She serves as an editorial director and is the author of several best-selling art books for children that are published by the Réunion des musées nationaux in France. These titles provide excellent introductions to the art of painting by focusing on themes such as colors, animals, children, numbers, and opposites. Her books are published and distributed in various languages and countries. Ms. Desnoëttes has received two major awards for *Le Musée des Couleurs (The Museum of Colors)* and *Le Musée des Contraires (Opposites)*.

Ms. Desnoëttes has also created a series titled *Balade en couleur.* The first two volumes are dedicated to the works of the French artists Edgar Degas and Auguste Renoir.

Ms. Desnoëttes is the author of *La Peinture au fil du temps (Painting As Time Goes By),* a history of painting over the course of 2,000 years, and *La Ménagerie extraordinaire (The Amazing Menagerie),* a book on sculptures of animals. *Les 5 Sens (The Five Senses),* her most recent book, concerns the discovery of the five senses in painting and sculpture.

In all of her publications, Caroline Desnoëttes seeks to introduce children around the world to the pleasures of learning to look at and discover art.

Colors of The Museum of Fine Arts, Houston is her first English-language title.

Dimensions for all works are given in inches.

*Cover: Paul Klee, **Marjamshausen** (detail), 1928, watercolor on paper, 14 3/16 x 8 1/16, Gift of Miss Ima Hogg.*

Color, like painting, is a source of beauty and pleasure.
By mixing the primary colors of yellow, red, and blue

the painter obtains new, complementary ones — orange, violet, green.

The painter organizes his palette with cold colors — violet, blue, and green —
and warm colors — yellow, orange, and red.

Then he adds white and black for light and shade.

And so, the painter can make an infinite number of color combinations
and give life to his pictures as light reveals the colors.